HACKING: THE NO-NONSENSE GUIDE

Learn Ethical Hacking Within 12 Hours!

Cyberpunk University

About Cyberpunk University

Cyberpunk University is one of the best sources of valuable ideas for computer programming and related courses. We have developed a wide range of simplified computer courses ranging from Introduction to programming to becoming an ethical hacker.

We have discovered the trick to teaching seemingly 'complex' computer courses to anybody with basic computer knowledge within half a day of study. We know how quite tricky it is to learn and master these skills and have gone the extra mile to ensure that the content we present is easy to understand and put into practice.

We are here to simplify the struggle faced by many when it comes to learning popular courses in computing, whether you are advancing your career in computer science or are a hobbyist looking to know more about how computers work. We find ways to make it easier for one to understand what it is all about and how to succeed in it.

Our team is comprised of professionals who have been in the computing and information industry of information technology for decades. The experience we have gained over the years is what enables us to create great guides and books that you can rely on for quality instructions.

The team is made up of background checked, experienced, friendly and approachable computer programmers who are always willing to share their vast knowledge on their chosen specialization. Here at Cyberpunk University, you can always be sure that you are working with right people.

Find out more about our other books in the series:

1. Python: The No-Nonsense Guide, Learn Python Programming Within 12 Hours!

2. Hacking: The No-Nonsense Guide, Learn Ethical Hacking Within 12

Hours!

To help you get the most out of this book we have created the **FREE** "**Hacking: The No-Nonsense Pro Tips**" infographic. The graphic contains the awesome "Newbie Hacking Index" which will help you with a quick overview of hacking essential jargon. Also included in the infographic, Security Tools the Pro's use in Kali Linux. We have uncovered the secret tools the Pro's use in order for you to get from Padawan to Jedi Master in a heartbeat!

DOWNLOAD THE FREE HACKING INFOGRAPHIC HERE:

http://hacking.cyberpunkuniversity.com/

CONTENTS

Hour 1:

Introduction to Hacking and Types of Hackers

When computers emerged as the mandatory devices to successfully run businesses, process personal data, and save information, it was only a matter of time before the society became wholly dependent on them for every aspect of life.

The emergence of the Internet marked a point of no return to the relationship that humanity has with machines. We now depend on computers for almost all types of communications, shopping, business, entertainment, and mainly to stay alive. This networking of computers to facilitate communication has however exposed our personal and business information to the outside world and cyber crime.

Cybercrime is the use of computers to commit fraudulent acts that may include privacy invasion, sabotage, fraud, and disseminating confidential information among others. Cybercrime has grown to become a very serious threat to people's lives and costs many individuals, organizations, businesses, and governments around the world billions of dollars every year.

Most people committing these cybercrimes are hackers. Paradoxically, the people that the victims of this crime need to protect themselves, their data, and information infrastructure against such attacks are also hackers... except they are a different kind of hackers.

Before we can dive deep into understanding hackers, first let us understand what hacking is.

1.1 What is hacking?

The definition of hacking is very broad. For the purpose of this book, we can define hacking as the process of finding weaknesses in computer systems and computer network systems and exploiting them to gain access to information.

We can, therefore, say that a hacker is a person who identifies and exploits weaknesses in computer systems and/or networks to access information. A hacker is typically a skilled computer programmer with knowledge of computer and network security.

1.2 Types of Hackers

The word hacker is usually synonymous with someone attacking a computer or computer network for malicious or selfish reasons, but that is not always the case. Now that we have established what a hacker does, we can classify them into four based on the intent of their actions.

White Hat (Ethical) Hacker

You are taking this crash course to become a White hat or ethical hacker. You will learn the skills and have the ability to gain access to computer and network systems to identify and fix weaknesses.

You will also perform various computing tasks such as vulnerability assessment and carry out penetration testing.

Grey Hat Hacker

Somewhere between a white hat (ethical) and black hat (criminal) hackers lies the gray hat hacker. This individual breaks into a computer or computer network system without prior consent from the authority to (or "intending to") identify weaknesses in the system and reveal them to the system owner for a reward or a job to fix the weakness.

Black hat (Criminal) Hacker

Also a criminal hacker, a black hat hacker is an individual who gains unauthorized access to a computer or network system for personal gain. A black hat hacker typically accesses a system to demonstrate his prowess in hacking, to violate policy rights, steal corporate data, etc. or deny legitimate users service.

Hacktivist

A hacktivist is a new type of hacker who uses his skills of penetrating a computer system or computer network driven by a social, political, humanitarian, or religious agenda. Hactivists, often in groups, typically hijack websites, social media accounts, and other platforms to send their messages.

Script kiddie

The term 'script kiddie' refers to an unskilled person who uses hacking tools available on the internet to penetrate a computer or network system. It can also be used to refer to a skilled hacker who chooses to use pre-written code or scripts to do the dirty work.

1.3 What is Cybercrime?

You have probably already heard of people being taken to court and jailed for committing computer crimes, increasingly being referred to as cybercrimes. All over the world, people are going to jail for creating and spreading computer viruses, bullying other people online, committing fraud, phishing, accessing classified information, and stealing corporate and user data.

Cybercrimes specifically refer to illegal actions committed over the internet. Some cybercrimes may also be carried out through telephone lines and mobile phones, on chat and social platforms, and on the location where the computer or network is physical. Here is a list of different types of cybercrime to help you understand better what constitutes it.

Computer fraud	Electronic funds transfer	Espionage
Privacy violation	Electronic money laundering	Data harvesting
Identity Theft	ATM Fraud	Phishing
Intellectual property theft	Denial of Service Attacks	Spoofing
Copyright infringement	Spam	Scamming

1.4 What is ethical hacking?

As we have explained earlier, hacking is the act of identifying weaknesses in a computer system or computer networks, then coming up with counter measures that can take advantage of the found weaknesses to penetrate the system. What sets an ethical and criminal hacker apart is the motivation behind the hack and not the process itself.

To be an ethical hacker, one must abide by the following rules:

1. Identify the devices or networks to hack or test and determine the hacking processes.
2. Get written permission from stakeholders of the computer or network before the hack.
3. Protect the privacy of the system and information of the organization being hacked.
4. Create a clear report of all the identified weaknesses and present to the organization.
5. Inform software and hardware vendors of any identified weaknesses in their products.

1.5 Do we need ethical hackers?

Private companies, organizations, government agencies, and individuals today are in constant need of ethical hackers as their first defense in protecting their computers and networks from the bad guys. The increasing use of computers in processing, transmitting, and storing information means that IT security needs more than just a steel door with a lock.

The primary purpose of an ethical hacker is to determine whether a client's computer or network is adequately protected. As information becomes, the most valuable asset organizations have, keeping it secure protects not only the interest and image of an organization but also safeguards the data integrity of their users.

Black hat hackers cause thousands of businesses millions of losses every year. Ethical hacking has emerged as a step ahead of the hackers that the organizations take to preempt and prevent attacks on their computer systems and information network. It is, therefore, justifiable to say that white hat hackers are the necessary tech-savvy guardians that individuals, businesses, and even governments can depend on to protect their interests.

1.6 Legality of ethical hacking

As long as the hacker abides by the five core rules of ethical hacking stipulated in section 1.4, the hack is considered legal if the stakeholders approved it in writing. The International Council of E-Commerce Consultants (EC-Council) offers a certification program that you can test your hacking skills, and if you are up to it, you get a recognized certificate. Note, however, that because of the rapid advancement in computer and information security, you will be required to renew the certificate after a while.

Hour 2:

Build your Kali Linux hacking environment!

Imagine how much easier hacking would be if you had all the tools you need pre-installed on your computer. Well, Kali Linux is a distro (distribution) that comes with over 300 tools that a hacker and any other computer professional will find very useful.

Part of becoming a hacker, whatever your motivations, is having all the tools at your disposal for when you need them. In this second hour of learning to be a hacker, we will figure out how to install a virtual machine on your Linux and run Kali Linux from it.

2.1 Caution for Beginners: Do not be 'that guy.'

It is natural for a beginner in hacking to want magic, just the way Hollywood has convinced us the way hacking should be. Sadly, there are no tools that you can just Google and download then press a few buttons, and you have access to the CIA servers. If hacking were this easy, then the hackers would not be the glorified geniuses that they are today. Do not be that guy that wants magic NOW and easily gives up when it takes even a little more effort and time to make magic happen.

The truth is, hacking is an art that requires skills that take years of learning and practicing. Where you are now is the first step, but remember everyone started here. Whether you have some experience in hacking or are a complete newbie, just as long as you are not completely new to computers or programming, then hacking methodologies will be simpler to grasp than you imagined.

In this section, you will learn how to install Kali Linux on your machine to have all your tools in one place if you do not already have it in your system. If you are new to Kali and would like to know what Kali is, you better take a few minutes to read the official Kali documentation on http://docs.kali.org/.

2.2 What is Kali Linux?

Kali is a Debian-based Linux distribution operating system that comes with a wide range of hacker tools from penetration testing to security auditing. The operating system is funded, developed, and maintained by Offensive Security, one of the most recognizable companies when it comes to information security training. Kali Linux was unveiled in March 2013 as top-to-bottom and extensive rebuild of the BackTrack Linux that adhered fully to the development standards of Debian.

The first step to being a good hacker is to set up a kind of laboratory with all the basic resources to practice your hacks. For us to run Kali Linux and take advantage of the hundreds of tools it offers, we will need another piece of software - a virtual environment that simulates a different computer within your computer.

In this case, we will use the VMware Workstation Player. There are of course other platforms that you can use including Oracle's VirtualBox, Microsoft's Virtual PC, KVM, Citrix, and Hyper-V. VMWare Workstation Player is free for non-commercial use, but while it has limited features compared to Workstation which is built for professionals, it has everything a budding hacker needs.

Step 1: Download the software you need

Before you get started, it is important that you understand how software virtualization works and find out if your computer meets the basic hardware requirements to virtualize an entire operating system. Because this e-book is about hacking, it will assume that you already have the know-how to view your system specifications and even download and install software.

The software you need to download to get started are:

1. VMware Player download here: http://www.vmware.com/products/player/playerpro-evaluation.html

2. Kali Linux download here: https://www.kali.org/downloads/ or

3. VMware images of Kali here: http://www.offensive-security.com/kali-linux-vmware-arm-image-download/

The VMware image of Kali Linux provided by Offensive Security allows you to use the operating system tools without having to create a virtual machine - it is ready to run from the Workstation Player.

Note that these software programs run on all the three major operating systems -- Windows 7/10, OSX, and Linux.

Once you have downloaded all the necessary software, unzip the files and place them in one directory you can easily access.

Step 2: Install VMware Station Player

Install VMware Player on your computer. After installation, you should easily start it by clicking on a shortcut on your computer's installed programs list. Here is what you should see:

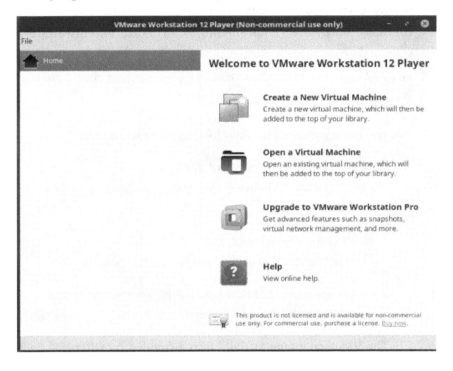

Fig 1: VMware Player start screen

The VMware player will present you with an option to create a new virtual machine, the option we will take for now, and the option to open a virtual machine, the option we will choose after we have set up Kali on the virtualization platform.

Step 3: Set up Kali Linux on VMware

Click 'Create a New Virtual Machine' on the VMware interface and select Installer disk image (iso). Browse to the directory in which you extracted the software you downloaded and find the Kali Linux ISO that you downloaded then click Next. Select the operating system Ubuntu for the system you are installing and choose a name for your virtual machine in the next window. I chose Kali.

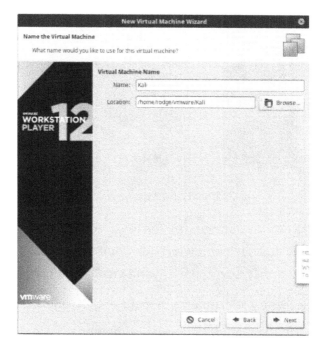

Fig 2: Setting up Kali Linux on VMware Player

In the next screen, set up the disk size for the new operating system to between 20 and 30 GB and select the option to store virtual disk as a single file.

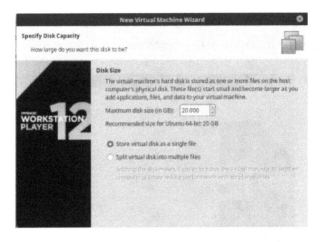

Fig 3: Specify Kali Linux disk options

Click Next to continue. In the next screen, you should see a summary of the set parameters for your new virtual OS. Click on Customize Hardware to make adjustments to the hardware profile.

The necessary adjustments to make in this window are:

Memory: Depending on your computer's RAM capacity, you should choose at least 512MB although 2GB would be ideal.

Processors: Leave this setting the way it is.

Network Adapter: Choose Bridged: Connected directly to the physical network.

Click Close to save the changes and click Finish to complete the setup. Here is what you should see on your VMware window:

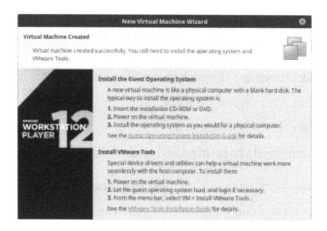

Fig 4: VMware Virtual Machine Created window

Your new machine running on Kali Linux OS is now ready to be installed.

Step 4: Install Kali Linux

When you launch the installation of Kali Linux on VMware, scroll down the options to Graphical Interface Install and press enter.

Fig 5: Installation of Kali Linux on VMware Player

Installation steps from this point should be pretty straightforward. The options you choose in every step are:

1. Select language (English in Fig 5).

2. Select your region/country.

3. Select the right keyboard.

Wait for components to be installed and configured.

4. Enter a hostname for the new machine.

5. Enter a domain name to configure the network.

6. Set up root password. Make sure to use a password you will remember.

Wait for user account details to be configured.

7. Select your timezone to configure the clock.

8. When prompted to partition disk, choose 'Guided - Use entire disk.'

9. Click Continue to install on the selected partition.

10. Choose to store all the files in one partition (recommended for new users).

11. Click Continue to effect the changes and confirm on the next screen.

Wait for the system to be installed.

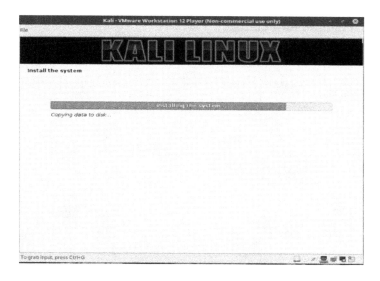

Fig 6: Kali Linux installation in progress

12. Select No to use a Network Mirror and click Continue to proceed.

13. Configure your Proxy if necessary and click Continue.

Wait for configuration to complete.

14. When prompted whether to install GRUB bootloader to the master boot record, click Yes then Continue and choose /dev/sda as the install location.

15. Installation should take up to 30 minutes to complete before the installation complete notification is displayed.

Wait for the system to complete installation and restart.

Step 5: Login to Kali Linux on VMware

After the system reboot, you should see a login screen like this:

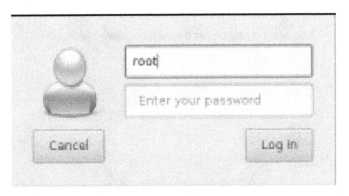

Fig 7: Kali Linux login screen

Use the following details to log in:

Username: root

Password: the password you set during setup

Congratulations!

You have successfully set up a fully-featured hacking environment powered by Kali Linux and running on VMware. When you log in, your workspace should look like this:

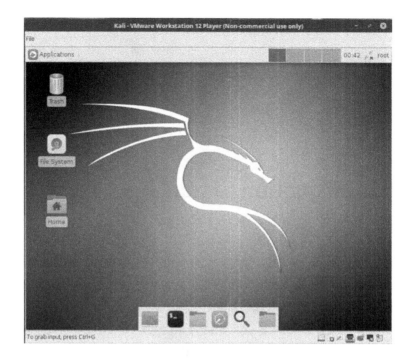

Fig 8: Kali Workspace

In the next hour, the real hacking begins!

Hour 3:

An Introduction to the Linux Terminal and CLI

This guide is streamlined for complete beginners in the Linux community to get on their feet and get started with the terminal, use the Linux command line (LCI), and execute commands. To become a hacker at all, especially if you intend to maximize on the tools that the Linux Kali offers, you must be good with the Linux command line. The standard way to interact with the Linux service is via the command line.

Learning the LCI may seem like a daunting task, but it is pretty easy if you master the basics and begin developing the skill on your own from there. This is why this guide, rather than present you a list of ready commands to enter into the terminal and get instant results, focuses more on describing the different elements of the terminal, how and why they work, and what you will use them for. Let's start.

3.1 The Terminal Emulator

A terminal emulator is essentially a program that enables you to use the terminal in a graphical user environment. Most people who are introduced to Linux are already familiar with other operating systems, mainly Microsoft Windows and Apple's Mac OSX which use a full graphical user interface to interact with the user in the day-to-day computer operations.

They, too, however, have terminal emulators you may have heard of: Terminal (default) and iTerm 2 in Mac OSX; and PuTTY in Windows. In Linux, it is necessary that you use the terminal emulator such as the default Terminal, XTerm, or KDE Konsole.

Each of these terminal emulators has its set of unique and shared features, and they are all great to work with and easy to use as you will learn.

3.2 The Shell

The shell in the Linux system is a command-line interface that interprets the commands and scripts that the user enters, then tells the operating system what to do with them. There are many shells that you will get acquainted with such as the Bourne shell (sh) and the C shell (csh). Each shell in Linux has its sets of features and intricacies when it comes to how they interpret commands, but they all share certain features: they all have input and output redirection, condition and variable testing, etc.

The default shell for most Linux distros including CentOS, Ubuntu, and RedHat is the Bourne shell, also known as bash, which is also what is used in this e-book. I should point out that this is also the default shell for

3.3 The Command Prompt

When you start the Terminal application on Linux, you will be taken to the command prompt or shell prompt, which is where you can enter the commands to issue to the computer. The information presented by the command prompt can differ depending on the version and distribution of Linux or how the user chooses to customize it. Typically, Ubuntu-based distributions have a command prompt in this format:

```
username@hostname~$
```

The tilde symbol (~) represents the current directory in bash, the default Ubuntu shell. This special character expands to the entire path of the current user's directory which in this case would be /home/username.

The prompt symbol ($) denotes the end of the command prompt after which the user's keyboard input cursor will appear. However, when you log into the command prompt as a superuser, the $ symbol will be replaced by #. Try entering this in your command prompt after the $ symbol then presses enter:

```
username@hostname~$ su
```

You will be prompted to enter your root password because you entered a command to switch to a superuser with root access. Once your enter your password, the command prompt will change to something like this:

```
hostname username #
```

The symbol (#) is the standard symbol for root. The root is a superuser account in Linux, which means it is a special account that can perform system-wide administrative functions and must be used with caution. This is a free user account with privileges to perform any task. It is recommended that you do not switch to a superuser account unless it is necessary. Instead, you can use the sudo command that we will learn in a short while.

3.4 Executing Commands

Commands are executed by the Shell when you specify the name of an executable file in the form of a binary program or a script file. There are thousands of standard Linux commands and utilities that come with the operating system that you can use to navigate the file system, install and configure software packages, and run the system and third-party applications.

A running instance of an executed command is called a process. When you execute a command in the foreground, which is the default state in which commands are executed, you must wait for the process to complete before you can revert to the command prompt to issue a new command.

It is important to understand that almost all commands in Linux, including file and directory names, arguments, and options are case sensitive. If you enter a command you know right, and it does now cause the effect you expected, the first thing you should do is double check the spelling and the letters case.

3.4.1 Execute commands without arguments or options

You can run a command without any arguments or options by simply typing the name of the command then hitting return. Running a command like this causes it to exhibit its default behavior, which is dependent on the command. e.g.

Cd	will bring your back to the current user's home directory.
ls	will print a list of the directories and files in the current working directory.
ip	will print how to use the ip command.

3.4.2 Execute commands with arguments

Many commands in Linux accept arguments, also called parameters, which have a direct impact on the behavior of the command. e.g.

cd /usr/bin	Argument specifies which directory to change to, in this case, bin directory inside usr directory.
ls /usr/bin	Prints a list of directories and files in the directory /usr/bin.

3.4.3 Execute commands with options

Most commands accept options, also referred to as switches or flags. These options modify the behavior of the command. Options follow a command and are indicated by one - character preceding one or more options represented by single uppercase or lowercase letters. Note, however, that some options start with -- followed by one character or a multi-character word that is typically descriptive of what the option does e.g.

ls -a	Prints a listing of directories and files including any hidden ones.
ls -l	Prints a long listing of files and directories including extra details.
ls -l -a	Prints a long listing of files and directories including hidden ones.

As you can see in the last example above, options can be grouped together. An alternative way to run the last command above is to combine options like this:

ls -la

3.4.4 Execute commands with options and arguments

As you get familiar with Linux, one thing you will quickly notice is that you can almost always combine options and arguments when running commands on the terminal. For instance, it is easy for you to check the contents of a directory regardless of the present working directory by just running this command

ls -la /home

In this ls command, -la are the options while the /home is the argument that points to the file or directory that the command can refer to.

3.5 More commands

This chapter introduces the basics of the Linux terminal and is in no way exhaustive. However, the foundation laid in this hour should help you expand your knowledge of Linux commands, how to navigate view, and edit files and their permissions — and to become a formidable hacker.

Here is a summary of some of the most popular commands you can practice to reinforce the idea of how commands work in Linux:

cd	Change to the home directory. Also used to navigate the Linux file system
pwd	(print working directory) Shows the path of the current working folder.
ls	Print a list of directories and folders in the pwd. Items are color coded such that: Blue are directories, White are text files, Red are archives, Cyan are Links, Green are Executable files, and Pink are image files.
cat	Displays the contents of a file. It must have a filename

	as an argument.
touch	Creates a new file. It requires a filename as an argument.
mv	Renames a file e.g. mv oldname.txt newname.txt.
cp	Copies a file from one directory to another. Requires source and destination arguments.
rm	Removes (Deletes) a file. Command expects filename as the argument.
find	Use this command to search for files within a directory. Requires directory path as well as filename as arguments.
lsblk	(List Block Devices) Prints block devices by their assigned names in a tree-like style on the standard output.
uname	(Unix Name) prints detailed information about your machine including machine name, OS, and Kernel.
history	(Event Record) prints a long history of commands executed in the terminal in the past.
sudo	(superuser do) allows a permitted user to execute commands with superuser privileges.
mkdir	(Make directory) create a new folder inside working directory.

Hour 4:

Using Tor and VPN to Stay Anonymous Online

As an aspiring hacker, one of the most important things that will make you exceptional in what you do is how well you cover your tracks on the internet. A hacker cannot afford to leave traces all over the place, not if they do not want to be caught. In this hour, you will learn how to be a ghost using two powerful tools: a virtual private network (VPN) and a Tor anonymity network.

A proxy hides your true identity and location by directing traffic to and fro your computer via one or more other computers. A proxy is like a web filter which applies proxy settings to data transferred by your browser.

There are public and private proxies you can use, with the private ones often costing a small fee but offering more stable service and dependability.

4.1.1 Why is a Proxy alone is not good enough for a hacker?

Proxies today primarily use SOCKS and HTTP which offers no encryption and SOCKS/HTTPS which encrypts data using SSL-quality encryption. This level of safety is not ideal for a hacker.

We will not focus on proxies in this e-book because it is just not safe enough for a hacker. One reason for this is that many proxies work by sending the user's original IP address to the destination site, which should be a concern for someone whose security and privacy are of primary importance.

Besides, proxies must be configured separately for each application that accesses the internet such as email app and third-party apps. Always remember that proxies only protect the browser traffic unless you configure every other application with web access (if they support proxy servers).

4.2 Anonymity and Privacy with VPN

VPN is an acronym for Virtual Private Network. This is a type of connection that creates a secure connection to a computer in another location, allowing your computer to appear as if it is in that place. It works by creating an encrypted virtual tunnel to a VPN server and makes all your browsing appear as if to come from it. When you set up a VPN, all your internet traffic will go through this encrypted tunnel, keeping all the information safe from eavesdroppers, other hackers, and pretty much everyone else.

One similarity between a proxy and a VPN is that you get to enjoy all the benefits of the remote server including speed, geographic location appearance, and encrypted data security.

Unlike a proxy server, a VPN service replaces all your ISP routing, routing ALL your traffic through the VPN server. This includes all application and system traffic. Also, while you have to configure proxy servers each time you want to use or disconnect a proxy service, with VPN, you can easily connect or disconnect with the click of a button.

4.2.1 Setting up VPN on Kali Linux

A. *Step 1: Enable VPN on Kali Linux*

Start Kali Linux by starting VMware then choose the appropriate file to load.

By default, the VPN section on Kali Linux is grayed out. To enable it, start the terminal right inside Kali and enter the following command:

root@kali:~# apt-get install network-manager-openvpn

In some cases, this may fail, and you may need to restart the network manager and try again to make it work. Restart the network manager using this command:

root@kali:~# service networking restart

B. *Step 2: Download and extract openvpn certs*

Still, on your Kali terminal, download the openvpn.zip file from http://www.vpnbook.com/ and save the archive in a location you can access with ease.

Once the download is complete, extract the contents of the file to the right directory. We are interested in the .ovpn file. Use the following command:

unzip -q [archive_filename.zip] -d /etc/openvpn

C. Step 3: Configure Network Manager to use the VPN

- Go to the Network Manager then click on Edit connections.

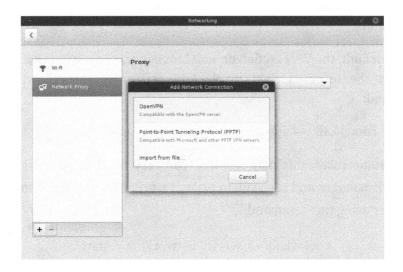

- Adding a new OpenVPN connection

Click on the VPN tab then click Add (+) and on the drop-down menu select type OpenVPN. Click Create. Choose import from file and navigate to the location of the extracted archive. You should find a file with .ovpn extension. Click on it to import.

- Find the username and password from
  http://www.vpnbook.com/.

On the new window, click on OpenVPN then fill up the following VPN details:

- Click Advanced then check the box to use LZO data compression.

- Click OK, then Save and Close to apply the changes.

Your VPN is now configured

4.3 Tor

Tor, derived as an acronym for its original software project name The Onion Router, is a free networking system that enables anonymous communication over the internet. It directs Internet traffic through a free, and global volunteer network made up of more than 6,000 relays to hide a user's location from anyone carrying out traffic analysis to those conducting network surveillance.

Using Tor makes it almost impossible for anyone to trace or intercept your Internet activity including websites visited and contents, online posts, chat messages, emails, and files shared. The system uses software that was designed specifically to protect the safety and privacy of the users and to promote freedom of communication by keeping users' Internet activities safe from third-parties.

4.3.1 Setting up Tor Browser on Kali Linux

The first thing you will do in setting up your Kali hacking environment is to download and install the Tor service. Start your emulator (VMware) then load Kali OS. When its state is restored, start the terminal and enter this command:

apt-get install tor

Wait for the operation to complete then download and install the Tor bundle from this link:

https://www.torproject.org/projects/torbrowser.html.en.

Be sure to download the right software for your computer architecture (32-bit or 64-bit). Also, be sure to change your current working directory to the downloads folder. You can use these commands:

cd /Downloads/

You can then use this command to extract the contents of the archive:

tar -xJf tor-browser-*

Once extraction is completed, change to the new directory, which should be named tor-browser and begin the installation process. The commands to use are:

cd tor-browser*

./start-tor-browser.desktop

You shouldn't run into problems running these commands logged in as a superuser. Some guides insist that you create a new user with limited privileges then run the installation using the sudo command. You can try this if the installation does not work for you or if you encounter errors.

Congratulations! You have installed the Tor service and browser.

4.4 Combining VPN and Tor

Modern-day security-conscious hackers who take no chances with online anonymity can set up and use both Tor and VPN on their computers. While this setup will dramatically slow down the connection largely because of Tor's many relays that data has to pass through before reaching the final destination, it is the safest possible way to send data over the internet securely.

There are two ways to go about using both VPN and Tor to anonymize your data online:

4.4.1 Tor through VPN

In this connection, first, you connect to your VPN server, then connect to the Tor network before accessing the internet. This is how your internet connection is routed when you use the Tor browser (which is less safe) or Whonix (safer) while connected to a VPN server. Your apparent IP on the internet will be the IP provided at the Tor exit node.

Your computer > VPN > Tor > internet

4.4.2 VPN through Tor

With this type of connection, first, you connect to the Tor network and then route your traffic through a VPN server to the internet. This setup requires that you configure your VPN client to work with Tor, which means you will have to find one that supports this type of connection. The best examples are AirVPN and BolehVPN. The greatest benefit of this setup is that you can get to choose a server location while still using the Tor network to stay anonymous.

Your computer > encrypt with VPN > Tor > VPN > internet

4.5 Final Thoughts on Anonymity

To use the Tor service, you must use the Tor browser.

Essentially, the browser is designed to point to the Tor nodes that are a special proxy relay servers that the network uses to anonymize data. If you browse using the Firefox or any other browser, you wouldn't be using the Tor service even if it is installed on your system.

Hour 5:

Hacking with Nmap

Nmap, an acronym for "Network Mapper," is an open source network exploration and network security auditing tool that you can use on Kali Linux. This tool was designed to swiftly scan computers in an extensive network just as efficiently as it does a single host.

It uses raw IP packets to discover details about hosts on a network including services, operating systems and their versions, types of packet filters or firewalls the use and a ton of other technical specifications.

Nmap is most popular among computer network security aficionados and systems and network administrators who use it routinely for tasks such as network inventory, monitoring hosts, and service uptime, and managing service and upgrade schedules.

In this hour, you will learn how you, as a hacker, can leverage Nmap to find vulnerable hosts in a network and hack them.

WARNING: Be very careful when using the aggressive functions of Nmap against hosts you do not have permission to scan. It may be against the terms and conditions of your ISP to use Nmap features.

5.1 Scanning Open Ports and Detecting Host OS with Nmap

In this section, we will learn how to scan for open ports and detect the operating systems of the target hosts using Nmap. First off, let us start by pinging an IP range to determine which live hosts are available.

Start Kali Linux on your VMware if it is not already running and start the Terminal emulator. Enter the following command:

nmap

The terminal will furnish you with a lot of useful information about this tool. Take some time to read it all because they are answers to questions you will have once you begin getting familiar with the tool.

Next, we will find a host IP or a range of host IPs to scan. In this example, I will use IPs I have permission to scan/hack. You should also find computers you have the authorization to experiment your new skills on. As a placeholder, we will use IP addresses 192.168.0.0 to 192.168.0.100 in this demonstration.

Type the following command, replacing the host IP or IP range with your own:

nmap -sP 192.168.0.0-100

We can also start the SYN scan and detect the operating system of the live host using the command:

nmap -sS 192.168.0.0 -O

This command will scan for more open ports and will display the operating system of the target host at 192.168.0.0. If you wish to scan the OS with version detection, you can use the command with these options:

Nmap -sV 192.168.0.0 -A

You can even increase the verbosity of the scan results by adding a -v option thus:

Nmap -sV 192.168.0.0 -A -v

5.2 Heartbleed SSL bug Scanning using Nmap on Kali Linux

The Heartbleed SSL Bug officially known as the CVE-2014-0160 is a serious vulnerability in computers that you can scan using the Nmap tool. The bug is in the popular OpenSSL cryptographic software library that was released back in 2012. This vulnerability allows an attacker to access and steal information protected by the SSL/TLS encryption, one of the most popular encryptions used to protect connections to the internet today.

Note, however, that since the bug was discovered, a fix has been developed and deployed by many operating system and application vendors. The objective of this section is to scan for computers whose Heartbleed SSL bug has not been patched and is therefore still available for exploitation.

Use the following command to scan a target host IP or a range of IP addresses:.

nmap -d –script ssl-heartbleed –script-args vulns.showall -sV [host]

By using the -script-args vulns.showall, you are essentially telling Nmap to show you which scanned targets are vulnerable and which ones are not.

The scanning of Heartbleed typically takes a few seconds, and the results are definitive. However, finding a vulnerability is one thing, exploiting it is another more complicated step.

As a hacker, you now can tell a client whether their computer is vulnerable to exploitation based on whether the systems in the network have been patched to fix the Heartbleed bug vulnerability.

5.3 Finding Live hosts with Nmap

For an ethical hacker, being able to detect hosts that are live is a very important capability that makes your work very easy. The Nmap tool is vital because you can use it to scan a network and find live hosts that you can further probe for vulnerabilities.

We will use Nmap together with ifconfig which will help us determine the range of IP addresses that the tool will scan for live hosts. Nmap will ping each host on the network within the specified range to determine whether it is live or not.

Enter the following command:

nmap -sP 192.168.0.0-100

Nmap will return a list of all the hosts detected within the range and whether the host is up or down.

If you would like to increase the verbosity of the ping scan, you can add -v option to return the list of hosts along with their statuses.

nmap -sP 192.168.0.0-100 -v

5.4 Nmap options summary

Nmap is a very powerful tool that you must continuously learn about to make use of fully. In this section, I will summarize the many options available to use with nmap to expand its functionality.

5.4.1 Host discovery options

-sL	(Scan List)- list of targets to scan
-Pn	Will Treat all hosts as online and skip host discovery
PS/PA/PU/PY[portlist]	TCP SYN/ACK, UDP or SCTP discovery
-PO[protocol list]	IP Protocol Ping
–dns-servers <serv1,[serv2],...>	Specify custom DNS servers
–system-dns	Use operating system's DNS resolver
-sn	(Ping Scan) – disables port scan
-PE/PP/PM	ICMP echo, timestamp, and netmask request host discovery probes
-n/-R	Never make DNS resolution, always resolve
–traceroute	Trace hop path to each host

5.4.2 Scan techniques

-sU	UDP Scan
-sO	IP protocol scan
-b <FTP relay host>:	FTP bounce scan
-p <port ranges>:	scan only specified ports
-sY/sZ:	scan SCTP INIT/COOKIE-ECHO
–scanflags <flags>:	Customize TCP scan flags
-sI <zombie host:[probeport]>:	Idle scan

5.4.3 Port specification and scan order:

–exclude-ports <port ranges>:	Excludes the specified ports from scanning
-r:	Scan ports consecutively not randomized
-F:	Fast mode that scans fewer ports than the default scan
–port-ratio <ratio>:	Scans ports that are more common than <ratio>
–top-ports <number>:	Scan <number> most common ports

5.4.4 Firewall evasion and spoofing

-f; –mtu <val>:	fragment packets
-e <iface>:	Use specified interface
-D <decoy1,decoy2,[ME],...>:	mask a scan with decoys
-g/–source-port <portnum>:	Use provided port number
-S <IP_Address>:	Spoof source address
–data <hex string>:	Append a payload to sent packets
–data-string <string>:	Append a ASCII string to sent packets
–proxies <url1,[url2],...>:	Relay connection through proxies
–ip-options <options>:	Send packets with included ip options
–ttl <val>:	Set IP time-to-live field

–badsum:	Send packets with bogus TCP/UDP/SCTP checksum
–spoof-mac <mac address/prefix/vendor name>:	Spoof your computer's MAC address
-data-length <num>:	Append random data to sent packets

5.4.5 Service and Version Detection

–version-intensity <level>:	Set from 0 (slight) to 9 (try all probes)
–version-all:	Try all probes (intensity 9)
–version-trace:	Show detailed version scan activity
-sV:	Probe open ports for service/version info

5.4.6 OS detection

–osscan-limit:	Limit OS detection to promising targets
-O:	Enable OS detection
–osscan-guess:	Guess OS more aggressively

Hour 6:

Cracking Passwords

Passwords. If only we know everyone else's, and no one knew our own.

The end user security in the hierarchy of information processing, the user, primarily keeps data safe on a computer using a password. But there just as there is a tool to pick any lock, there is a tool to crack (almost) any password. In this section, we will highlight two very potent and very modern tools that hackers use to find passwords.

6.1 Cracking Passwords with John the Ripper

Let me introduce you to John the Ripper. This free password cracking tool was initially built for the Unix operating system. It works so well that it is now available on over 15 different platforms.

John Ripper is a password testing and breaking app that combines various cracking techniques (or packages) that autodetect password hash types and even has a customized cracker. It is a formidable tool to use or try to break many types of encrypted password types used on Unix-based operating systems. Extendability features such as MD4-based passwords and hashes stored in LDAP or MySQL makes John the Ripper the most popular tool used by blackhat and whitehat hackers.

Step 1: Preparation

The Linux operating system stores passwords in a shadow file inside the /etc./ folder. For this exercise, we are going to create a folder, save it in that location, then attempt to crack it using John the Ripper. We will create a new user 'admin' for the Linux Kali system with a simple password **'password123.'**

```
root@kali:~# adduser happy
Adding user `happy' ...
Adding new group `happy' (1001) ...
Adding new user `happy' (1000) with group `admin...
Creating home directory `/home/admin' ...
Copying files from `/etc/skel' ...
Enter new UNIX password:
Retype new UNIX password:
passwd: password updated successfully
Changing the user information for happy
Enter the new value, or press ENTER for the default
        Full Name []:
        Room Number []:
        Work Phone []:
        Home Phone []:
        Other []:
Is the information correct? [Y/n] y
root@kali:~#
```

Step 2: Unshadowing password

Next, we will use the unshadow command to combine the data inside the /, etc/shadow and /etc/password to end up with a single file with the password and username details of the user account we will attempt to crack using John the Ripper. We will name the file usr.

```
root@kali:~# unshadow

Usage: unshadow PASSWORD-FILE SHADOW-FILE


root@kali:~# unshadow /etc/passwd /etc/shadow > ~/usr
```

Step 3: Crack the password with a wordlist

The new file will be cracked by John the Ripper. We will use the password list that comes with the tool on Kali Linux. The password is list stored in the directory:

usr/share/john/password.lst

In the future, you will be able to generate your wordlist to use to crack a user password. Enter the following command:

```
root@kali:~# john --wordlist=/usr/share/john/password.lst ~/usr

Loaded 2 password hashes with 2 different salts (sha512crypt
[64/64])

Password123        (admin)

guesses: 1  time: 0:00:00:21 DONE (Wed Jan 11 07:21:08 2017) c/s:
300  trying: sss

Use the "--show" option to display all of the cracked passwords
```

John the Ripper was able to crack the hash to find the password 'password123' for the user 'admin.' This was possible because the password 'password123' was one of the possible passwords in the Passwords list. If the actual password were not on the list, the crack would have failed.

Step 4: Cracking a password without a wordlist

It is possible to use John the Ripper to crack a password without providing a list of possible passwords. As a budding hacker, you will want to try and see if this method actually works.

On your Kali terminal, enter the following code to remember:

```
root@kali:~# john ~/filename
```

The /filename in the code demo above represents the file where the user password is stored.

According to the documentation on http://www.openwall.com /john/doc/MODES.shtml, John the Ripper will try the 'single crack' mode first and if it does not work, use an available wordlist with rules, and if this is not successful, switch to 'incremental' mode.

I should point out that your installation of Kali Linux comes with another password cracking tool called Ncrack. To find it, navigate to Kali Linux's list of tools by clicking on Application > Password attacks. Ncrack is right there. It is described as a high-speed network authentication cracking tool that was designed to help companies secure their networks proactively by testing all their network and network devices for poor passwords. You can read more about this tool on http://tools.kali.org/password-attacks/ncrack.

6.2 Cracking Passwords with Hydra

Best known as 'THC-Hydra', hydra is a powerful online password attack tool that uses brute force and other password cracking combinations on live internet services such as http, https, smtp, snmp, ssh, smb, and telnet among others. This tool supports over 30 protocols including those secured with SSL and brute forces services using wordlists and userlists.

Hydra has four working modes:

i. One username One password mode.
ii. Userlist and one password mode.
iii. One username and password list mode.
iv. Userlist and password list mode.

What makes Hydra one-of-a-kind password cracking tool is that it is a fast connection bruteforcer that is also flexible with tons of new modules always available to add with ease. There are lots of password lists out there that a hacker such as yourself will get familiar using, you can find them with a simple Google search.

6.2.1 Understanding Hydra Command

For a brute force kind of password cracking to work, no matter which tool you use, you need to have a list of possible passwords that the software will use. You can also use a list of passwords that comes with John the Ripper - it is pretty much the same thing.

You can find Hydra on Kali Linux by going to Applications >Password Attacks > Online Attacks > Hydra. When you click it, it should open on the terminal. Alternatively, you can easily use the command hydra on the terminal to initiate this tool.

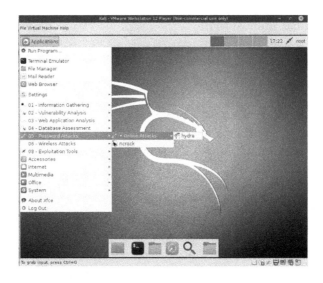

If Hydra is not pre-installed on your version of Kali Linux, you can set it up by entering:

apt-get install hydra-gtk

Hydra uses the following command for a typical basic attack:

Hydra -l username -p passwordlist target

The username is a single username such as "user" or "admin" or can be a list of usernames. The passwordlist is typically a text file that contains the possible passwords to match the username, and the target is the service or host to that authenticates the credentials. The target can be an IP address and port number or a specific web form field.

You can check the passwords that come with Kali Linux default in the directory /usr/share/wordlists by first going to the directory:

root@kali: ~# cd /usr/share/wordlists

Then listing the contents of the directory:

```
root@kali: /usr/share/wordlists# ls

Dirb        fasttrack.txt    metasploit-jtr w3af.txt

Dirbusterfern-wi-fi      metaspoilt-pro       salmap
```

To use hydra to crack a password, use the command format illustrated in the previous page, replacing the placeholders username, passwordlist, and target with actual information. For instance, an attack would be structured like this:

```
root@kali: /usr/share/wordlists# hydra -l admin -p
/usr/share/wordlists/mypasswords.txt 192.168.0.0 8080
```

6.2.2 Using Hydra on web forms

There is a level of complexity in using Hydra on web forms because you have to provide more information parameters that the form needs. However, the syntax is pretty much the same as above.

To use hydra on a web form, you will need the URL, form parameters, and failure string instead of the IP. This means your command would be structured like this:

Hydra -l username -p passwordlist <url>:<formparameters>:<failure string>

Unfortunately, using Hydra on a webform is beyond the scope of this book. We could go into detail with demonstrations and examples, but this tool alone would need an entire book to cover how you can use it to hack into Facebook, Gmail, or any other formidable online service.

The most critical of the parameters required to crack an online web form using Hydra is the failure string. This is the text that the form returns when Hydra attempts incorrect username and, or password combinations. This information is vital because Hydra needs to know when an attempt fails so it can move on to the next attempt.

You can read more and discover the many features, and practical examples of using Hydra and its advanced features on the Kali Linux web page here: http://tools.kali.org/password-attacks/hydra.

Hour 7:

Using the Harvester and DMitry to Gather Information

Being a hacker is essentially being an information harvester. There are many ways to gather information even before the actual hacking begins. Some practical Hollywood movies and shows have shown us how hackers can go through trash cans to gather as much information about their targets.

You would be surprised how simpler hacking a person, or their computer is when you collect bits of information about themselves that they leave all over the place, and especially on the internet.

7.1 Information Gathering Using the Harvester

This hour is all about information gathering through footprinting and scanning. These are among the most important preparation steps that can make the difference between a successful penetration and a failed test. Considering that information is a weapon, you need as much information about the client and the network for a successful hack.

7.1.1 about the Harvester

Developed in Python by Christian Martorella, TheHarvester is a tool that you use to gather information about email accounts, usernames, and hostnames and subdomains from various public sources such as social media, search engines, and PGP key servers.

The Harvester is designed to be used at the earliest stages of penetration testing. It is a simple but highly effective tool that supports a range of sources including:

- Google (emails, hostnames, subdomains, Google+ profile employee names)
- Bing (Emails, hostnames, subdomains, virtual hosts)
- Pgp servers (emails, hostnames, subdomains)
- LinkedIn (employee names)
- Exalead (emails, hostnames, subdomains)
- Twitter
- Yahoo
- Baidu
- Shodan

7.1.2 Installing the Harvester

Initialize your Kali Linux OS inside the virtual environment then download the harvester by going to this address on the browser:

https://github.com/laramies/theHarvester

Download the repository folder then extract the contents somewhere easily accessible, such as the desktop. Unzip the contents of the archive onto the desktop using the command:

unzip theHarvester.zip

The contents of the will be inflated on to the desktop in the folder theHarvester.

Next, provide an execute permission for theHarvester.py using chmod command below. Remember to switch the working directory to the theHarvester directory.

chmod 755 theHarvester.py

Once this is done, theHarvester is ready to run using the command theHarvester. You should see detailed information including the version of theHarvester and other options.

7.1.3 Using theHarvester

One of the best things about theHarvester is that its command syntax is rather basic. Using it to gather information is not as complicated as many other hacking processes and tools such as cracking passwords and hacking Wi-Fi networks, which typically have as many as ten steps.

The first step in using theHarvester is initializing the program from the shell. You can do this by typing:

#theharvester

Here is an outline of theHarvester's command syntax:

#theharvester -d [domain] -l [results_limit] -b [data_source]

When you use the above query on your chosen domain, theHarvester will return a list of email addresses depending on the limits you set in [results_limit]. You can then choose the HTML file to save the results, and where to save the file for further reference using the parameter -f.

For instance, if you were to run a query on a workplace's website to gather email addresses of all the employees, you could use this syntax:

#theharvester -d companywebsite.com -l 100 -b google

That is pretty much it. With this simple command, theHarvester will crawl all over the internet snatching up all information that fit the criteria you specify.

You can also carry out a search of the information you want on all search engines at once using the option -all in place of the [data_source]. Your syntax would then look like this:

#theharvester -d companywebsite.com -l 100 -b all

7.1.4 More theHarvester Options

Besides limiting the maximum number of results the number of results and the source of data, there are some excellent parameters and options that you will find useful as you master the art of data gathering using theHarvester. These include:

-s:	Start in result number x. The default is 0.
-v:	Verify the host name using DNS resolution and search for any virtual hosts.
-n:	Carry out a DNS reverse query on the ranges discovered.
-c:	Carry out a DNS brute force for the specified domain name.
-t:	Carry out a DNS TLD expansion discovery.
-h:	Use shodan database to query the hosts discovered.
-e:	Use this DNS server.

7.2 Information Gathering Using DMitry

DMitry (Deepmagic Information Gathering Tool) is a command line application coded using the C language that you can use to gather as much information as possible on and about a host. This tool's base functionality is to gather information on email addresses, subdomains, system uptime information, domain whois data, and tcp port scans, etc.

7.2.1 Setting Up DMitry

You can run DMitry from the Kali Linux shell or you can use the downloadable GUI application. To download DMitry using the shell, use the following command:

 # wget http://mor-pah.net/code/DMitry-1.3a.tar.gz

Use the following commands to install the tool:

 # tar xzvf DMitry-1.3a.tar.gz

 # cd DMitry-1.3a/

 # ./configure

 # make

 # sudo make install

If you would rather use the GUI application, you can download the latest version 1.3a from one of these links:

*   http://mor-pah.net/software/dmitry-deepmagic-information-gathering-tool/

*   ftp://ftp.freebsd.org/pub/FreeBSD/ports/packages/security/dmitry-1.3a.tbz

*   https://github.com/jaygreig86/dmitry/

When the download is complete, you can then install the FreeBSD package on Kali Linux.

7.2.2 Using DMitry

You can start DMitry from the Terminal using the command:

dmitry

If you installed the GUI application, you will find a shortcut to the tool under:

Application> Information Gathering> Live Host Identification > dmitry

Simply click on the link, and the app will start.

Just like theHarvester, DMitry has a rather basic command syntax. For instance, to carry out a whois lookup of a host IP address, simply enter the command in this format:

dmitry -i [IP_address]

For example, to look up the whois information of the IP address 192.168.0.1, you would enter:

dmitry -i 192.168.0.1

You will use -w when performing a whois lookup of a domain name.

dmitry -w companywebsite.com

To carry out a search for possible subdomains on a domain name, you will use the -s command. The syntax will look like this:

dmitry -s companywebsite.com

Use -p in the command syntax to carry out a TCP port scan on a target IP address. The command would look like this:

dmitry -p 192.168.0.1

When you want to carry out a TCP port scan on a host and filter the output report, use the -f command. This is particularly important to identify which ports are protected by a firewall and which ones are not. You must add -p to this command to successfully scan and filter the results. Your command would look something like this:

dmitry -pf companywebsite.com

The -e command is used to carry out a search for all email addresses linked to a domain name. The command syntax looks like this:

dmitry -e companywebsite.com

Use the -n command to find netcraft information about a host (check out netcraft.com). This will include uptime information where available. The command should look like this:

dmitry -n companywebsite.com

To save the output results you find using dmitry, use the -o command and specify the filename. If not specified, the default name will be host.txt

dmitry -e companywebsite.com -o company_emails.txt

7.3 Conclusion

I cannot emphasize strongly enough how important information gathering is to the whole process of hacking. When you carry out proper reconnaissance by collecting all the information you can about a host, it will increase the chances of finding vulnerabilities in a system, hence saving you time and effort.

There are quite a number of great tools you should know about including:

a) Parsero (leverages information contained in the Robots.txt file of web servers.)

b) Wireshark (analyzes network protocols. It is very popular with corporations and educational institutions.)

c) ntop (shows in-depth network usage information.)

d) Casefile (built for offline use.)

e) Maltego (used to scan for network vulnerabilities and finding IP addresses.)

Hour 8:

Using the Nessus Vulnerability Scanner in Kali

Nessus is one of the most comprehensive network security vulnerability scanner by Tenable Network Security. It is one of the most popular client-server framework tools used by hackers and widely deployed by information and computer security experts.

This tool is available as a software package that you can install on your computer or as a pre-configured VM. The wide variety of plugins that Tenable has is that makes Nessus such a great tool that can interface with almost any networked device. This hour, we will figure out how to install and set up Nessus and how you can use it to scan for vulnerabilities in a target host.

8.1 Features of Nessus

Nessus has many tools that support penetration testing activities that you will need, especially if you pursue hacking beyond the basics. They include:

- It scans for and identifies vulnerabilities that allow you to access a computer system's information.
- It checks the system for any known but unpatched vulnerabilities in computer software.
- It tries logging into hosts, services, and accounts using common and defaults passwords.
- Carries out configuration audits, vulnerability analyses, and mobile device audits, and reports them in customized formats.

8.2 Downloading and Setting Up Nessus on Kali Linux

On your Kali Linux browser, go to http://www.tenable.com/ products/nessus/select-your-operating-system to download Nessus. Select the right operating system (Debian 6, 7, 8 / Kali Linux 1 AMD64) then agree to the terms of service for the download to begin. The file is about 36 megabytes.

When the download is complete, the next step is to install it from the shell. Initialize the terminal then change the working directory to the location of the downloaded .deb package.

Use the following command to install the package:

dpkg -i Nessus-6.9.3-debian6_amd64.deb

If the file you downloaded has a different name or version, be sure to rectify it on the command line. The installation process should begin.

Once the installation is complete, you should see a message that all plugins have been loaded and tips on how to start Nexus as well as where to configure your scanner. Note these two details because they are important.

8.3 Initializing Nessus

The first thing we will do is get a Nessus license, an activation code that we will use down the line. On your browser, go to https://www.tenable.com/products/nessus/nessus-plugins/obtain-an-activation-code and register for a free Nessus Home activation code.

Enter the following command on your Kali shell to start the back-end Nessus server:

 # /etc/init.d/nessusd start

You will need to use this command every time you start Nessus on Kali Linux. You should see a message:

"Starting Nessus:"

The nest step is to set up Nessus. On your browser, go to:

https://127.0.0.1:8834

You should get a message that the connection is not safe or the certificate invalid. Just accept the self-signed cert and proceed to the Nessus page where you will see a welcome message. Click continue to create a login ID to use the scanner.

Note the username and password you choose because you will need it later to log into the front-end of Nessus scanner.

In the next screen, you will be prompted to enter the activation code. Choose to register Nessus (Home, Professional or Manager) and enter the activation code that was emailed to you then click continue. If the secret activation code is valid, Nessus should then automatically connect and begin downloading updates as well as the latest plugins. Note that it might take a while.

Nessus is fetching the newest plugin set

Please wait...

8.4 Using Nessus

You will be prompted to enter the login details you created earlier when the download is complete. Load the web interface, and the page will automatically take you to the Scan Queue. Because Nessus is a straightforward tool, scanning for vulnerabilities is easy. You will find almost everything you need right on the top menu of the application.

On the Scan Queue, on the sub-menu to the right of the page, click New Scan to open a New Scan Template page. This is where you will set up your scan target. Give the new scan an appropriate name then select Run Now and under policy select Internal Network Scan.

Under the Scan Target, you will enter the IP address of the host you want to scan or enter multiple IPs separated by commas. Nessus also allows you to scan an address range such as 192.168.0.1-100 or an entire subnet such as 192.168.0.1/24. When done filling the template details, click Run Scan at the bottom of the page and Nessus will do its thing.

Important tip: Users familiar with Nessus report that this tool may crash highly vulnerable targets. It is, therefore, important that you run a scan on a host that you have specifically set aside to test the tool. As a white hat hacker, I cannot emphasize enough how important it is that you only scan targets that you own or those that you have permission to scan. Nessus is a potent tool that you should never play around with.

You will automatically be taken back to the Scan Queue page when the scan begins. On this page, you can keep track of the progress of the scan and any other scans in progress. If you want to see more details about the scan, you can click on the scan in progress to view the progress on the Summary page. Note that the information on the summary page may not be automatically refreshed.

When the scan is complete, the Summary page will contain the details of the scan including the individual summaries of all the hosts you entered in the Scan Target field of the Scan Template. This information will be saved such that you can access it later by simply clicking on the Results tab on top of the page.

The scan summary will contain information about the scanned targets including all the vulnerabilities discovered in the host scanned. When you click on the host, you will be able to see an even more specific listing of the vulnerabilities discovered along with brief explanations of the information gathered during the scan.

When you click on vulnerability information, it will take you to a page with even greater details about the vulnerability including descriptions and Security Bulletin Numbers. Nessus often lists Windows-specific vulnerabilities by this number that corresponds with known vulnerabilities within Metasploit. This will make it easy for a hacker to easily find out how such a vulnerability analysis can be turned into an exploit.

8.5 Conclusion

You have had a first-hand experience using Nessus to scan for vulnerabilities on a target host. You should understand now why Nessus is the most trusted and preferred scanner on the market. It is simple to use, accurate, and reliable. The results are very detailed and exploiting found vulnerabilities is easier with Security Bulletin numbers when you scan a Windows host.

In the future, when you want to extend your vulnerability scanning, you can upgrade to the Nessus Manager or Nessus Cloud tools to have even more potent tools at your fingertips. Tenable also has several other great tools that you should discover including the Security Center Continuous View and the Passive Vulnerability Scanner which are used by IT organizations to put in place continuous monitoring solutions and to gather operational and vulnerability data through scanning, logging, and sniffing.

Hour 9:

Wireless Hacking: Things You Should Know

For a hacking to take place, there must be a communication connection between at least two devices, and the connection between them can be via a cable (LAN) or wireless. Most hacking processes you have learned so far are done over the internet, meaning that they have been remote hacks that you can carry out anywhere provided the target host is online, and you have an internet connection.

The kinds of hackers you hear about on the news causing so much trouble to your potential clients are remote hackers. However, there is an even more dangerous type of hacker who can compromise a computer system by finding vulnerabilities in local computers using the client's wireless network. More and more corporations and even individuals are hiring whitehat hackers to try to hack their wireless systems to know just how safe you are.

In this and the next hour, we will cover wireless hacking. This chapter will cover all the important things you need to know about wireless networks to prepare you for the different kinds of networks you will encounter and how easy or difficult it is to hack each one. You will learn what hidden networks are and find out how much of a challenge they are to a hacker. This hour is meant to give you a rough idea on how different kinds of wireless networks are usually hacked.

9.1 Understanding Wireless Security Levels

Wireless networks can be classified according to how secure they are. The various wireless network security protocols will need different hacking strategies, but first, let us summarize how many there are:

9.2 Open Wireless Network

A public wi-fi is a free wireless network that is typically available to the public to connect to the access point (wireless router) and access the internet. There are two types of open wireless networks:

9.2.1 Open unrestricted

This is a kind of network where anyone can connect to and use without limitations. This is the kind of network used in public places such as trains, restaurants, and Wi-Fi hotspots that offer free internet access.

9.2.2 Open but restricted

With this kind of network, users can connect to the access point, but this does not guarantee access to the internet. This kind of connection has another layer of authentication beneath the open protocol.

Considering that hacking a wireless network refers to finding the router's password, you can hack the open but restricted but not the open, unrestricted network. However, in the scope of this book, both of these networks do not require hacking.

9.3 WEP (Wired Equivalent Privacy) Wireless Networks

Picture this as a house that asks you for a password before the door opens for you. Using tools that come with Kali Linux, you will be able to hack this type of network within minutes because WEP is the least secure security protocol. ISPs who require users to log in to access the internet on their network, schools and colleges that require students to log in with their student ID and password to access the internet and large offices still use this security protocol. However, WEP is less common today as security-conscious network admins prefer WPA and WPA-2.

9.4 WPA (Wi-Fi Protected Access) Wireless Networks

The development of the WPA and later WPA-2 security protocol was a direct response to the apparent vulnerabilities that WEP standard had. WPA was officially adopted in 2003, just a year before the WEP was officially retired. The most common configurations of WPA is Pre-Shared Key (WPA-PSK) which features a 256-bit encryption system that can either use TKIP (Temporary Key Integrity Protocol) or AES (Advanced Encryption Standard).

As far as security goes, the TKIP is an earlier a stopgap encryption protocol that is no longer considered secure because it is easier to hack. This means that as an ethical hacker, you will have an easier time with a TKIP Wi-Fi than AES.

The AES was introduced with WPA-2 as a replacement for TKIP in WPA, and it is considered so secure that even the US military uses it.

9.5 Hidden Networks

Any type of Wi-Fi networks we have discussed can be hidden. Consider it "security through obscurity." A hidden network does not broadcast its name (called SSID) and is, therefore, a little bit harder to access or hack. It is a lot like trying to pick a lock to a door you do not know where it is located.

Kali Linux comes with several tools that you will use to scan for and find hidden network SSIDs.

You have two options to find a hidden network: passive and active. With the passive method, you can wait until a client connects to the network to locate the network from the clues the client leaves behind. The active method involves de-authenticating clients on the network to force the access point to reveal the network details. However, finding and hacking hidden wireless networks is not the scope of this book.

9.6 What Makes WPA Networks so Secure?

Some of the changes implemented in WPA that makes it more secure than WEP include message integrity checks, which are carried out to determine whether an intruder had intercepted or altered packets exchanged between a client and the access point.

The WPA-2 protocol that was launched in 2006 introduced Counter Cipher Mode with Block Chaining Message Authentication Protocol (CCMP) which is essentially what makes the AES more secure than the TKIP.

One of the top weakness of the AES is brute-force attacks, which can be prevented by using strong and complex passphrases. The Wi-Fi Protected Setup (WPS) remains the biggest hole in the WPA armor because an intruder just needs to gain access to the secured Wi-Fi network to access the keys they need to hack devices on the network.

In summation...

Now that you have a general idea of the various types of wireless network security protocols, you are better armed to learn how to hack a Wi-Fi network. In the next hour, we will get our hands' dirty learning to hack WPA and WPA-2 Wi-Fi networks.

Hour 10:

Hacking WPA/WPA-2 Wireless Networks

I will be straight with you and say that hacking a WPA/WPA-2 network is a tedious and most cases time consuming job. In some cases, a dictionary attack may take days, and even then it may not be a success. Also, the best dictionaries you will need to download are huge files. This is so because a brute force or dictionary attack is a trial-and-error approach to establish a connection with an access point using different combinations of all the letters of the alphabet in both upper and lower case, numbers, and common symbols.

Rainbow tables, which are known to speed up the hacking process by completing parts of the letter, number, and symbol combinations, is a large file that could be hundreds of gigabytes. This hour, we will learn two of the most effective ways to hack a wireless WPA or WPA-2 network to introduce you to the world of on-location wireless penetration.

10.1 Hacking WPA/WPA-2 WPS Using Reaver

WPS (Wi-Fi Protected Setup), which was introduced to complement the WPA, is designed to be easier to configure but tough to crack. However, it has a well-known security hole that various tools such as Reaver can exploit with minimal effort on your part. Note, however, that it still might take hours for the hack to be successful, but as you will discover later in the hour, it is a much more preferable technique than brute force.

10.1.1 Information Gathering

Before you can begin using Reaver on Kali Linux to hack a WPA/WPA-2 protected the wireless network, you first need to know whether WPS is enabled. This attack will not work if WPS is not enabled. You will also need to know the BSSID of the network which means it would probably be best not to attempt this exercise on a hidden network.

Start VMware, load Kali Linux OS on the virtual machine and log into your root account.

Next, set the wireless interface to monitor mode using the following command:

airmon-ng start wlan

This command should reveal details of the adapter card interface, chipset, and driver as well as enable monitor mode as in the screenshot below.

Step 3: We can then use the wash command to find networks with WPS enabled. While wash is an easier way to detect a network, it might sometimes fail to detect networks even those with WPS enabled. The good thing is that any network it finds has WPS enabled. Here is the command:

wash -i mon

The results you get will contain a column of the network's BSSID.

Step 4: Use the airodump-ng to show all the networks around you and see which ones have WPA enabled. The command is:

airodump-ng mon

Step 5: Write down or copy the BSSID of the target network in the format XX:XX:XX:XX:XX:XX. This is what we need to hack the network using Reaver.

10.1.2 Hacking the Wireless Network

Step 6: Start Reaver on the terminal and begin the hack using the following command

root@kali # reaver -i mon -b [BSSID]

Replace [BSSID] with the network's BSSID you copied in the previous step. In the command, the -i is the interface to use, which is the network monitor mode we created in step 4. The -b in the command specifies the BSSID of the target network.

That is all you need to do to initiate the hack. Depending on how secure the network is, the process may be over in a few minutes, or it might take hours. Be patient and let Reaver do its thing.

When the hack is complete, Reaver will present you with the password of the network in the message:

WPA PSK: [password]

If yours did not work as expected, read on to troubleshoot.

10.1.3 Known Issues with Reaver

1. It is not uncommon for Reaver to keep switching interfaces forever rather than carrying out the actual scan. If yours does this, try turning the wireless adapter on then back on then attempt the hack again.

2. Errors such as "Something went wrong with the wireless card," "AP does not use WPS," "You are too far from the AP," and "AP is choosy, does not let you associate" are straightforward and

have possible workarounds.

3. If you are using the version of Reaver that came bundled with your version of Kali Linux, you might want to update it first if it does not work. A newer version of Libpcap may solve the problem.

4. Reaver may not work if you have other services using the wireless adapter. For instance, if you are already connected to a Wi-Fi network, you may want to disconnect and refresh the AP before giving it another try.

5. If after many attempts and rectification of issues the hack does not work, perhaps the target network just isn't vulnerable. There are many other hacking tools available on the Kali platform that you can try.

10.2 Hacking WPA/WPA-2 Using Brute Force

Brute force is a very popular way to hack a secured wireless network because it takes advantage of users' susceptibility to create easy and textbook passwords. If you find that a network's WPS is secure and Reaver is not getting anywhere, brute force, also called dictionary or wordlist attack may work. There are many tools you can use on Kali Linux, but for this guide, we will use the Hashcat tool.

10.2.1 What is the Hashcat Tool?

The Hashcat is a CPU-based tool has been around for quite some time. The Hashcat tool we will use uses modern GPU processors to crack encrypted username and password hashes on WPA and WPA-2 wireless networks.

Step 1: Capturing a 4-way handshake with the router

First, you will need to capture a 4-way handshake with the secured wireless network and save it in a .cap file. Your network adapter must support monitor mode, just as with the previous hack. We will use the airmon-ng command to switch to monitor mode and airodump-ng to sniff the networks. Enter the following commands on your Kali Linux shell:

airmon-ng start wlan0mon

airodump-ng wlan0mon

airodump-ng -c 1 -b XX:XX:XX:XX:XX wlan0mon -w write2file

When the airodump-ng is done saving the file, send de-authentication packets to the target network access point to force connected devices to disconnect from the AP. You will then be able t capture the 4-way handshake when the devices are establishing a new connection using aireplay-ng. Here is the command to use:

aireplay-ng --deauth 100 -a [Router_Mac] -c [Device_Mac] wlan0mon

Replace [Router_Mac] with the router mac address and [Device_Mac] with the mac address of a connected device. If this attempt fails, retry several times because it is not uncommon for the first couple of attempts to fail. Just remember that the -a switch in aireplay-ng is for the Wi-Fi/AP mac address and -b is the mac address of the device connected to the wireless network.

Step 2: Convert the .cap file to .hccap

Hashcat works with a .hccap file while the data we need is stored in a .cap file. Use the following command to convert the file and assign it the name handshake.hccap:

aircrack-ng filename.cap -J handshake.hccap

Step 3: Download a wordlist to use in the hack

One of the best things about Hashcat is that it creates its own wordlist to use in the brute force hack on the fly. This means that you can use it without downloading an existing dictionary of passwords to try. We will cover this in Step 5, but for now, we will get ready with a downloadable wordlist.

There are many wordlists you can download on the internet in .txt files. A simple Internet search should give you millions of results. Simply filter results to find the newest hosted in a credible site and download it. However, be sure to check that the wordlist is created specifically for WPA/WPA-2 as the passwords must be eight characters long. Save the file in root, where the handshake.hccap file is located.

Step 4: Use oclHashcat with a wordlist

Use the following command to crack the WPA handshake file, which is now in the .hccap format:

oclhashcat -m 1000 /root/handshake.hccap /root/wordlist.txt

At this point, you can let Hashcat run the hack attempts in the background. Depending on the speed and memory of your GPU, this tool can peak at over 150,000 attempts per second. You can tweak the command using -u to get fill speed.

Step 5: Use oclHashcat without a wordlist

Alternatively, you can let Hashcat create its own dictionary on the fly and not clog it up with a massive wordlist. For this to work though, you will need to use various masking options in order to create a text file with your prefered charsets. The basic set include:

?u = ABCDEFGHIJKLMNOPQRSTUVWXYZ

?l = abcdefghijklmnopqrstuvwxyz

?d = 0123456789

?s = !"#$%&'()+,-./:;??@\^`{|}~

?a = All the above characters (?L, ?U,?D, and ?s)

Other character sets and switches available on Hashcat include:

?l?l?l?l?l?l?l?l = a-z, 8 Characters long.

?u?u?u?u?u?u?u?u = A-Z, 8 Characters long.

?d?d?d?d?d?d?d?d = 0-9, 8 Characters long.

?s?s?s?s?s?s?s?s = All special characters, 8 characters long.

?a?a?a?a?a?a?a?a = a-z, A-Z, 0-9, and all special characters, 8 characters long.

Hashcat offers you the option to choose an attack mode to use. The switches to use are:

0 = Straight attack

1 = Combination attack

3 = Brute force attack

6 = Hybrid dictionary + mask attack

7 = Hybrid mask + dictionary attack

For instance, to carry out a mask brute force attack, you will use the -a 3 switch

10.3 Conclusion

Hacking a secured network is not easy, and this explains why it takes long even when successful. However, with so many hacking tools available on the Kali Linux platform, you will discover a pattern and even your favorite methods with practice in your lab. These two approaches are basically examples of how you would go about using almost every other WPA/WPA-2 hacking tool in your arsenal.

Hour 11:

Web SQL Injection

One of the top risks to information and computers on the internet today is SQL injection. Hackers use this technique by exploiting a security vulnerability in the database layer of a web application, which can be found when the user input is not correctly filtered for string literal escape characters that are embedded in SQL statements.

Understanding how to detect and identify web SQL injection risks on a client web application early enough is very critical. In this hour, we will walk through the steps of identifying the database vulnerabilities and the SQL commands that are inserted into a website's URL string or data structures to retrieve a response that will allow us to infiltrate a web application. Web SQL injection is often very effective on web pages that are developed using PHP and ASP.NET.

If successful, an SQL injection should allow you to dump an entire database of a system, modify the content of the database, or carry out various queries that the web application would otherwise not let you perform.

11.1 Finding a Target Web Page

As we have learned in the previous hours of this book, the first and most important step of any hack attack is preparation. Preparation for an SQL injection attack primarily involves finding a vulnerable target. This can be quite time consuming process, sometimes even taking longer than the actual attack. More and more websites are now better protected from this kind of hack. Hence the reason finding a vulnerable target could take very long.

The easiest and most effective approach to finding out whether a web page is vulnerable is called Google Dorking. In this case, a dork is a specific search query that searches for and finds websites that meet the specified advanced query parameters that you input. Some of the dorks that you can use to find websites that are vulnerable to an SQL injection attack are:

> inurl:index.php?id=
>
> inurl:trainers.php?id=
>
> inurl:buy.php?category=
>
> inurl:article.php?ID=
>
> inurl:play_old.php?id=
>
> inurl:declaration_more.php?decl_id=
>
> inurl:pageid=
>
> inurl:games.php?id=
>
> inurl:page.php?file=
>
> inurl:newsDetail.php?id=
>
> inurl:gallery.php?id=
>
> inurl:article.php?id=
>
> inurl:show.php?id=
>
> inurl:staff_id=

inurl:trainers.php?id=

inurl:buy.php?category=

inurl:article.php?ID=

inurl:play_old.php?id=

inurl:pageid=

inurl:games.php?id=

inurl:page.php?file=

inurl:newsDetail.php?id=

inurl:gallery.php?id=

inurl:article.php?id=

inurl:show.php?id=

inurl:staff_id=

inurl:newsitem.php?num=

inurl:index.php?id=

inurl:declaration_more.php?decl_id=

inurl:newsitem.php?num=

There are of course many other dorks you can use, simply search online and you will be bombarded with hundreds of these queries.

These search queries share a key component: that they all focus on websites that use PHP scripts to generate dynamic content based on entries in an SQL database stored on a server somewhere. While a good hacker could attack and infiltrate any website that uses an SQL database, almost anyone can hack PHP-based websites because most are set up by just about anyone. A good example is WordPress websites that are often installed by novices who are not keen to test their websites and ensure that they are injection-proof.

11.2 Testing a Web Page for Vulnerability

Google will return millions of results of web pages meeting any of the criteria you use to find a target. However, this does not mean that all the dorks are vulnerable to SQL injection attacks. You must then test each site until you find one that is vulnerable to attack. An excellent way to do this is to use the " ' " character (apostrophe) in a string on the page's URL to see if it returns an error.

If the web application does not properly validate the input that contains the apostrophe correctly before it is passed to an SQL statement, then it is possible to hack the SQL database.

Assuming that one of the web pages in our results is website.com when we enter, enter an apostrophe at then do the target page URL like below and press enter:

http://www.website.com/index.php?id=1'

What does the page return? If you see a SQL error, it means that the website is vulnerable and you could try an SQL injection attack. If the page loads normally with no errors, it is not the candidate you are looking to hack, and you can move on to the next page on your URL list.

It does not matter what error you get, as long as you get an error, the page is a good candidate for an SQL injection attack. From here, it is important that you understand SQL to be able to manipulate the database directly right from the vulnerable page.

11.3 Carrying Out an SQL Attack

Let us assume that our target, website.com/index.php?id=1. The next step is to find out how many columns the SQL database has and how many of them can accept queries you will use. Append the statement "order by" to the URL such that it appears like below:

http://www.website.com/index.php?id=1 order by 1

Start with 1 after "order by" and keep increasing the number until the page returns an error. When you see an error, it means that you will have exceeded the maximum number of columns the database has. For instance, if you get an error when you get to "order by 8", it means that the database has 7 columns.

The next step is to find out which columns can accept queries, hence open to exploitation. You can do this by adding a hyphen (-) before the 1 after id= and then append the statement "union select" to the URL, much like the "order by" statement in the previous step, except with a list of columns to make this process faster. Your new URL should look like this:

http://www.website.com/index.php?id=-1 union select 1,2,3,4,5,6,7

This query will return the list of column numbers that can accept database queries from you. Note these columns to inject the SQL statements.

11.4 Exploiting the SQL Database

Once you determine which columns to direct your SQL queries at, you can then begin the actual hack of the database. From this point on, you will rely on union select statements to carry out the attack. If you are not familiar with manipulating SQL databases, perhaps this is the time to get a crash course to be able to exploit the vulnerable SQL database.

Some of the most common functions you can query including listing all the databases available, finding out the ID and username of the current user, finding out the names of all or vulnerable columns, and which data types they accept. Note that the columns are where the web pages store all website information including customer names, email addresses, last login times, etc.

11.5 Conclusion

This demonstration of SQL injection hack that you carried out on a web page you have permission to hack is a clear demonstration that you need no special knowledge or tools to infiltrate information on an insecure web page on the internet. But that is not all; it can get even easier.

The SQLMAP tool that comes bundled with your Kali Linux (assuming you did not download the light version) is built to find such vulnerabilities with even greater ease and speed. You can download it for free from sqlmap.org if your version of Kali Linux does not have it or if you use a different operating system.

SQLMAP can scan web pages and send header requests to determine which ones are vulnerable to SQL injection then present you the list in a silver platter. It is fun to use it, especially if you plan on being a more proactive white hat hacker who does this more often.

Hour 12:

Executing a Remote Buffer Exploit with Python

If you know computers well enough to understand how computer programs are written and how they work, you will agree with me that Python is a brilliant language. It is a language that you can use to create dynamic and very useful tools just by stringing together [mostly] English phrases that even a newbie can understand. It is regarded as the lazy programmer's language that can produce little scripts of a handful lines of code that can do so much.

This hour, we figure out how you can use Python to create hacking tools that make your work easier and automate many of the exploits and penetration tests that you have learned over the past half day and those you will explore and learn as you work towards becoming the best ethical hacker the world has ever seen.

12.1 Python for Hackers: A Shortcut into Programming

At Cyberpunk University, we are committed to offering valuable knowledge that you will find beneficial beyond the basic satisfaction of curiosity. You have invested hours in learning the various tactics that seasoned hackers use every day, but you should know that this is just the beginning.

In our Python programming book "Python: The No-Nonsense Guide," we go in-depth to introduce Python as the programming language of the future. The most skilled hackers, both those who do it for fun, as a career, or for their selfish purposes (read: blackhat), are all programmers first. If you are not a good programmer, this is the perfect opportunity for you to learn to be one using the easiest and most versatile language there is and get to apply it to something practical and fun, such as hacking.

You could still be a good hacker without learning to write Python scripts, but you would essentially be a script kiddie. No one wants to remain a script kiddie forever, but it is a good enough place to start. So, here we go.

If you do not have Python installed on your computer, I suggest you download and install it. You can set aside the VMware virtual environment that you use to run Kali Linux for this hour.

You can download the latest version of Python interpreter version 3.6 (or 3.5) and a text editor (to write your code) before you begin. If you are completely new to Python, I would suggest you pause this hour first and get our Python eBook to learn all the basics before you are proficient enough to proceed with the next exploit.

12.2 What is a Remote Buffer Overflow Exploit?

If you have ever come across the term "Buffer overflow," chances are it was a reference to a vulnerability in a specific software or script. In information science, buffer overflow vulnerability refers to a programming error that results in a memory access exception.

A buffer overflow occurs when a process in the program attempts to store data that exceed the maximum limits of a fixed-length buffer, hence overwriting data contained in adjacent memory locations including the program's 'flow data.' This causes the process to terminate with a Segmentation Fault Error.

When there is a Segmentation Fault Error, that is to say when the data overflows to the next instruction location. It is possible to take control of that instruction via the execution flow and inject arbitrary commands into the system to process. In this hack, you will write a Python script that triggers this error and injects commands you specify so that you can take control of the host or simply find out what you want to know about a process in the memory location the data overflows too.

12.3 Preparation and Setup

At this point, you should have already learned all the basics about programming in Python, especially what the different data types are, how to write Python scripts, save .py files, and run the scripts. You should have Python 3 installed in your system (Linux or Windows are fine), and you should have an active internet connection. This exploit uses a TCP internet connection.

First off, we need to find a server to test our exploit on. As with every exercise in this guide, we insist that you only test this exploit on a machine you have permission to test on. Attempting to carry out hacks on strangers' computers over the Internet is illegal and could have very serious legal repercussion. Do not try it.

Finding a server to try your buffer overflow hack will be a bit of a challenge, but there are resources on the internet that you can use to find the right dork. You can begin by checking out the Google Hacking Databases provided by the good folks at exploit-db on https://www.exploit-db.com/google-hacking-database/ for live servers available to hack or for vulnerable software you can test your skills on.

12.4 Writing the Python Script

Once you find a server to try the buffer overflow hack on, the next step is much more fun: writing the code. We will first import the sys and socket libraries, then write the code to execute.

Start your text editor and enter the following code:

```
#!/usr/bin/python
import sys
import socket
for carg in sys.argv:
    if carg == "-s":
    argnum = sys.argv.index(carg)
    argnum += 1
    host = sys.argv[argnum]
    elif carg == "-p":
    argnum = sys.argv.index(carg)
    argnum += 1
    port = sys.argv[argnum]
buffer = "\x41" * 2500
s = socket.socket(socket.AF_INET, socket.SOCK_STRAEM)
s.connect((host,port))
s.send("USV " + buffer + "//r//n//r")
s.close()
```
print ("Overflow buffer exploit successfully sent!")

Here is what this Python does:

The first line imports the system library while the second imports the socket library that the script needs to run. The script will create a buffer with the value \x41 and multiplies it 2,500 times and sends it to the socket, which is declared as s. The buffer connects to the socket and sends the string USV, the new value of the buffer (which is 2500 times the value of \x41 before closing it. The script will display the message in print when the process is a success.

12.5 Executing the Remote Buffer Overflow Exploit Script

After you have saved the script, the next step is to execute it. Start Python (from the terminal or command prompt by typing Python and execute the script by switching the working directory to the location of the .py file. If you are unsure how to do this, it is all explained in detail in the Python ebook.

Congratulations! You have successfully written your first Python script exploit and executed it. You can also use Python to automate the many exploits we have studied in this ebook including the SQL injection hack we looked at in the last hour and the Nmap hack we saw on the hour 5.

12.6 Conclusion

Many people learn to hack computers out of sheer curiosity, just to discover if they can do it. Yes, anyone with the basic knowledge of computers can do almost all the hacks we have looked at so far. However, it takes a lot more effort, learning, and practice to figure out how to find other and new vulnerabilities and the best place to start is to learn how to write computer programs.

Learning to code with Python is the perfect place to start. You will also need other prerequisite computer skills including understanding of how most operating systems work (they are written in C/C++; hence you should find out what makes these languages stand out) and how computer networking works. The topics we have covered this hour and in this book are proof enough that hacking is not rocket science.

If you haven't already we highly suggest you get the Hacking infographic to get the most out of this book.

DOWNLOAD THE FREE HACKING INFOGRAPHIC HERE:

http://hacking.cyberpunkuniversity.com